Kabuliwallah

RABINDRANATH TAGORE
Kabuliwallah

TRANSLATED BY ARUNAVA SINHA

Illustrated by Mohit Suneja

ALEPH BOOK COMPANY
An independent publishing firm
promoted by *Rupa Publications India*

First published in India in 2024
by Aleph Book Company
7/16 Ansari Road, Daryaganj
New Delhi 110 002

This edition copyright © Aleph Book Company 2024
Illustrations copyright © Aleph Book Company 2024

Translation copyright © Arunava Sinha 2024

All rights reserved.

This is a work of fiction. Names, characters, places, and incidents are either the product of the author's imagination or are used fictitiously and any resemblance to any actual persons, living or dead, events, or locales is entirely coincidental.

No part of this publication may be reproduced, transmitted, or stored in a retrieval system, in any form or by any means, without permission in writing from Aleph Book Company.

ISBN: 978-81-19635-20-7

1 3 5 7 9 10 8 6 4 2

Printed in India

This book is sold subject to the condition that it shall not, by way of trade or otherwise, be lent, resold, hired out, or otherwise circulated without the publisher's prior consent in any form of binding or cover other than that in which it is published.

My five-year-old daughter talked all the time. It had taken her a year after her birth to master the language, and since then she has not wasted a second of her waking hours in silence. Although her mother often hushed her, this was beyond me. A silent Mini was so unnatural a being that I could not bear it for long. So I always encouraged her to prattle on.

I had barely started the seventeenth chapter of my novel that morning when Mini appeared by my side and began chattering at once, 'Ramdayal, the doorman, calls the crow kauwa instead of kaak. Baba, he just doesn't know anything, does he?'

Before I could talk about linguistic diversity, she had moved to another subject. 'Baba, Bhola says it rains because elephants spray water with their trunks from the sky. He talks such rubbish, my god. He keeps talking, talks all the time.'

Without pausing for my opinion, Mini suddenly asked, 'What relation is Ma to you, Baba?'

'Shaali,' I answered to myself. To Mini I said, 'Go play with Bhola, Mini. I'm busy.'

Flopping down by my feet, next to the desk, she began to play a game involving her knees and hands, accompanied by a rhyme uttered at express velocity. In the seventeenth chapter of my novel, Pratap Singh was about to leap with Kanchanmala in his arms from the high window of the prison into the river flowing below.

My room looked out on the street. Mini

abruptly stopped her game to rush to the window and began to shout, 'Kabuliwallah, Kabuliwallah.'

A tall Kabuliwallah—one of those hawkers of dry fruits who came all the way from Afghanistan to make a living in Calcutta—was walking slowly up the road, a turban on his head, a bag slung over his shoulder, holding two or three boxes of grapes. It was difficult to say what emotions he aroused in my daughter, but she continued to call out to him breathlessly. I was afraid that if the wily peddler, with a bag of things to sell, came into my room, I could bid goodbye to any prospect of finishing chapter seventeen that day.

The Kabuliwallah turned and smiled at Mini's shouts and began walking towards our house. Her courage gave way, and she ran from the room at great speed, vanishing into the house. She was convinced that if the

Kabuliwallah's bag was opened and examined it would reveal three or four children, just like her.

Meanwhile, the man himself appeared, offering me a smiling salute. Although Pratap Singh and Kanchanmala were in dire straits, I reflected that it would be discourteous to invite him into the house and buy nothing.

I bought a few things, and we began chatting. We exchanged notes on frontier policies involving Abdur Rahman, the Russians, and the English.

When he was about to leave, the Kabuliwallah finally asked, 'Where did your daughter go, Babu?'

I sent for Mini in order to dispel her fears. Pressing herself to me, Mini cast suspicious glances at the Kabuliwallah and his large bag. He offered her some raisins and dry fruit, but she simply wouldn't accept them, holding

my knee tightly. And there the first meeting between them ended.

A few days later, about to leave the house on an errand, I discovered my daughter seated on the bench next to the front door, chattering away with the Kabuliwallah who sat at her feet, listening smilingly, and occasionally saying something in broken Bengali. Mini had never encountered such an attentive listener in the five years of her life, besides her father. I even found nuts and raisins bundled into the aanchal of her tiny sari. 'Why have you given her all this?' I asked the Kabuliwallah. 'Don't do it again.' Taking an eight-anna coin out of my pocket, I handed it to him. He accepted it without demur, putting it in his bag.

I returned home to find the eight-anna coin at the heart of a hundred rupees worth of trouble.

Holding a circular, silvery object in her

hand, Mini's mother was asking her daughter disapprovingly, 'Where did you get this?'

'The Kabuliwallah gave it to me,' Mini told her.

'Why did you have to take it from him?' Mini's mother inquired.

'I didn't want to, he gave it on his own,' Mini said, on the verge of tears.

I rescued Mini from imminent danger and took her outside.

There I learnt that it wasn't as though this was only Mini's second meeting with Rahmat, the Kabuliwallah. He had been coming to see her almost every day, bribing her with almonds and raisins to conquer her tiny, greedy five-year-old heart.

I observed that the two friends had established an easy familiarity between themselves, sharing private jokes and quips. For instance, on spotting Rahmat, my daughter would ask, laughing, 'What's in that bag of yours, Kabuliwallah?'

In an exaggeratedly nasal tone Rahmat would answer, also laughing, 'An elephant.'

The joke could not be termed particularly subtle, but nevertheless it kept both in splits—and the artless laughter of a middle-aged man and a child on an autumn morning brought me some joy, too.

They had another ritual exchange. Rahmat would tell Mini, 'Khnokhi, tomi sasurbaari kakhanu jaabena. Little girl, you must never get married and go to your father-in-law's house.'

Most girls from traditional Bengali families would be familiar with the word shoshurbaari almost from the time they were born, but because we were somewhat modern, we hadn't taught our daughter the meaning of the term. So, she did not know what to make of Rahmat's request, but because it was against

her nature to be silent and unresponsive, she would fire a counter-question. 'Will you go there?'

Rahmat would brandish his enormous fist against an imaginary father-in-law, and say, 'I will kill the sasur first.'

Imagining the terrible fate awaiting this unknown creature, Mini would laugh her head off.

∫

It was the clear season of autumn. In ancient times, this was when kings set off to conquer other lands. I had never been anywhere outside Calcutta, but precisely for that reason my mind wandered all over the world. In the quiet corner of my room, I was like an eternal traveller, pining for places around the globe. My heart began to race as soon as another country was mentioned, the sight of a foreigner conjured up a vision of a cottage amidst rivers and mountains and forests, and thoughts of a joyful, free way of life captured my imagination.

But I was so retiring by nature that the very notion of abandoning my corner and stepping out into the world made me have visions of the sky crashing down on my head. That was why my conversations with this man from Kabul, this Kabuliwallah, every morning by the desk in my tiny room served the purpose of travel for me. Rugged and inaccessible, the scorched, red-hued mountain ranges rose high on either side of the road, a laden caravan of camels winding along the narrow trail between them; turbaned traders and travellers, some of them on the backs of camels, some on foot, some with spears, others with old-fashioned flint guns…with a voice like the rumbling of clouds, the Kabuliwallah would recount tales

from his homeland in broken Bengali, and these images would float past my eyes.

Mini's mother was perpetually jumpy, her mind alive with imaginary fears. The slightest noise on the streets would lead her to believe that all the inebriated individuals in the world were rushing towards our house, bent on making mischief. Despite all the years (not too many actually) she had lived on earth, she had still not rid herself of the conviction that the universe was populated only by thieves and robbers and drunkards and snakes and tigers and malaria and earthworms and cockroaches and white men all intent on striking terror into her heart.

She was not entirely free of doubt about Rahmat, the Kabuliwallah, requesting me repeatedly to keep an eye on him. When I attempted to laugh away her suspicions, she would ask me probing questions. 'Aren't children ever kidnapped? Don't they have slaves in Afghanistan? Is it entirely impossible for a gigantic Kabuliwallah to kidnap a small child?'

I had to acknowledge that it was not entirely impossible but unlikely. The capacity for trust was not the same in everyone, which was why my wife remained suspicious of the Kabuliwallah. But I could not stop Rahmat from visiting our house for no fault of his.

Rahmat usually went home around the end of January every year. He would be very busy collecting his dues at this time. He had to go from house to house, but still he made it a point to visit Mini once a day. There did seem to be a conspiracy between them. If he could not visit in the morning, he made his way to our house in the evening. It was true that I experienced a sudden surge of fear at the sight of the large man in his loose shalwar and kurta, standing in a dark corner of the room with his bags. But when a laughing Mini ran up to him, saying, 'Kabuliwallah, Kabuliwallah,' and the simple banter of old was resumed between the two friends of unequal age, my heart was filled with delight once more.

∽

I was correcting proofs one day in my tiny room. The cold had grown sharper; as winter was about to bid farewell, there was a severe chill. The morning sunshine filtering through the window warmed my feet; it was a most pleasant sensation. It was about eight o'clock—most of those who had ventured out for their morning constitutionals, their heads and throats wrapped in mufflers, were already back home. Suddenly, there was an uproar in the street.

Looking out of the window I saw two policemen frogmarching our Rahmat, bound with ropes, up the road, followed by a group of curious urchins. Rahmat's clothes were bloodstained, and one of the policemen held a dagger dripping with blood. Going out, I stopped the policemen to enquire what the matter was.

The story was related partly by a policeman and partly by Rahmat himself. One of our neighbours owed Rahmat some money for a shawl from Rampur. When he disclaimed the debt, an altercation broke out, in the course of which Rahmat had stabbed him with his dagger.

The Kabuliwallah was showering expletives on the liar when Mini emerged from the house, calling out, 'Kabuliwallah, Kabuliwallah.'

Rahmat's expression changed in an instant to a cheerful smile. Since there was no bag slung from his shoulder today, they could not have their usual discussion about its magical contents. Mini asked him directly, 'Will you go to your father-in-law's house?'

'That's exactly where I am going,' Rahmat smiled back at her.

When he saw Mini wasn't amused, he showed her his arms bound with rope. 'I would have killed the sasur, but my hands are tied.'

Rahmat was in jail for several years for causing grievous bodily harm.

We forgot him, more or less. Going about our everyday routines it didn't even occur to us how difficult it must be for a man used to roaming free in the mountains to cope with years of imprisonment.

Even Mini's father had to accept that his fickle-hearted daughter's behaviour was truly shameful. She effortlessly forgot her old friend, and struck up a new friendship with Nabi, who groomed horses. Then, as she grew older, male friends were replaced by girls her age. Now, we seldom saw each other any more.

Many years passed. Another autumn arrived. My Mini's wedding had been arranged. She would be married during the Durga Puja holidays. Along with the goddess from Kailash, the joy of my house would also depart for her husband's home, robbing her father's house of its light.

A beautiful morning had dawned. After the monsoon, the freshly rinsed autumn sunlight had taken on the colour of pure, molten gold. Its glow washed over the crumbling houses of exposed brick in the neighbourhood, making them exquisitely beautiful.

The shehnai had begun playing in my house before the night had ended. Its notes were like the sound of my heart weeping. The plaintive melody of Bhairavi was spreading the imminent pain of parting all over the world. My Mini was to be married today.

There had been a great to-do since the morning, with crowds of people going in and out of the house. In the courtyard a marquee was being set up with bamboo posts; the clinking of chandeliers being hung up in the rooms and the veranda could be heard. It was very noisy.

I was going over the accounts in my room when Rahmat appeared and saluted me.

I did not recognize him at first. He had neither his bags nor his long hair—his body was not as strapping as it once used to be.

It was his smile that eventually told me who he was.

'Why, it's Rahmat,' I said. 'When did you get back?'

'I was released from jail yesterday evening,' he answered.

His reply made me uncomfortable. Until now, I had never seen a murderer in the flesh, his presence here made me shrink back. On this auspicious day, I wished he would go away.

I told him, 'There's something important going on at home, I am busy. You'd better go today.'

At this he made ready to leave at once, but when he had reached the door, he said hesitantly, 'Can't I meet Khnokhi?'

He probably thought that Mini had not changed. Perhaps he expected her to come running up as before, chanting 'Kabuliwallah, Kabuliwallah', as she always had. To honour the old friendship he had even gone to the trouble of collecting a box of grapes and some nuts and raisins wrapped in paper from a fellow Afghan as he no longer had his own sack of goods to sell.

'There are some ceremonies at home today,' I told him, 'meeting Mini is impossible.'

He looked very disappointed. He looked at me wordlessly for a few moments, then said, 'Salaam, Babu,' and left.

No sooner had he left than I felt bad and was considering calling him back when I found him returning of his own accord.

Coming up to me, he said, 'I have some grapes and nuts and raisins for Khnokhi, please give them to her.'

As I was about to pay for them, he caught hold of my hand firmly and said, 'Please don't pay me. You have always been so kind, I will never forget your kindness....

'I have a daughter back home just like yours, Babu. It was thinking of her that I brought some fruit for Khnokhi, this isn't business.'

Putting his hand inside his long, loose shalwar, he pulled out a dirty piece of paper. Unfolding it carefully, he spread it out on my desk for me. It had the print of a tiny pair of hands. Not a photograph, not an oil painting, just some lampblack smeared on the palms to make a print on paper. Rahmat travelled to Calcutta's streets every year to sell his dry fruits, holding this remembrance of his daughter close to his breast—as though the touch of those tiny tender hands comforted the heart inside his broad chest, a heart wracked by the pain of separation.

Tears sprang to my eyes. I forgot that he was a seller of dry fruits from Kabul and I, a member of a Kulin Bengali family. I realized that he was a father, just as I was.

The handprint of his little Parbati from his home in the mountains reminded me of Mini.

I sent for my daughter at once. They raised objections in the ladies' chambers, but I paid no attention. Mini appeared shyly in my room, dressed as a bride in her red wedding garb.

The Kabuliwallah was taken aback when he saw her. Unable to revive their old banter, he said nothing for a while. Finally, he said with a smile, 'Khnokhi, tomi sasurbaari jaabis?'

Mini knew now what the words meant, she could not respond as before. Blushing at Rahmat's question, she stood with her face averted. I remembered the day Mini and the Kabuliwallah had met for the first time, and felt a twinge of sadness.

After Mini left, Rahmat slumped to the floor with a sigh. He had suddenly realized that his own daughter must have grown up and that he would have to get to know her all over again—she would no longer be the way he remembered her. Who knew what might have happened to her over these past eight years? The shehnai kept playing in the calming sunlight of the autumn morning, but inside a house in a Calcutta lane all that Rahmat could see were the mountains and cold deserts of Afghanistan.

I gave him some money. 'Go back home to your daughter, Rahmat,' I told him. 'Let the happiness of your reunion with her be a blessing for my Mini.'

Giving Rahmat the money meant pruning one or two things from the celebrations. The electric lights display was not as lavish as I had wanted it to be, nor were the musical arrangements as elaborate as planned. The ladies as usual objected strongly but, for me, the festivities were brightened by the benediction of a father's love.